Original title:

The Cool Breeze of Paradise

Copyright © 2025 Creative Arts Management OÜ
All rights reserved.

Author: Elias Marchant
ISBN HARDBACK: 978-1-80581-611-9
ISBN PAPERBACK: 978-1-80581-138-1
ISBN EBOOK: 978-1-80581-611-9

A Tapestry Woven in Air

A gentle gust tickles my nose,
It sweeps through the flowers and blows.
The daisies giggle, swaying in grace,
While squirrels do a dance, keeping pace.

The sun winks down, a cheeky fellow,
Bouncing off clouds, bright and yellow.
As if the sky's about to break,
With laughter and joy—the universe's prank!

I see the leaves in their quirky spin,
Trying to catch a breeze with a grin.
A butterfly flutters, in jest it flits,
Wearing a crown made of tiny bits.

Each whiff of air tells jokes untold,
Filled with giggles, big and bold.
In this place where whimsy does reign,
Laughter erupts like a whimsical train!

Revelry in Whispering Vales

In valleys where the giggles play,
A breeze tickles trees in a merry sway.
The squirrels dance with such delight,
Spinning tales till the fall of night.

A rabbit's hop turns into a jig,
While gossiping bees buzz in a twirl so big.
The flowers laugh in colors bright,
As the sun winks, oh what a sight!

Echoes of Tranquility

Where laughter floats and echoes soar,
The trees play hide and seek galore.
A playful breeze whispers silly songs,
As shadows stretch and dance along.

A ticklish leaf falls like a joke,
Landing softly near a happy oak.
The clouds chuckle, shapes they spin,
A whimsical race, let the fun begin!

Mystical Motion of Sweet Winds

When gentle gusts play hide and seek,
The flowers whisper things unique.
Petals flutter in a funny chase,
As each breeze can't find its place.

The sunlight giggles, dances bright,
Painting rainbows in sheer delight.
As butterflies join in with cheer,
It's a carnival, oh dear, oh dear!

Floating Dreams on a Soft Draft

In a zephyr's laugh, dreams take flight,
Kites weave through with colors so bright.
Fish chase clouds in the azure sea,
While ants celebrate with a tiny spree.

The shadows play tricks on the grass,
As time just floats by like a glass.
With every twist of the night's sweet haze,
The world's a circus as it sways.

Tranquil Airs of Eden

In the land of plump green trees,
Where birds chatter blooper melodies,
A squirrel steals a nap on a cloud,
While a goat shouts jokes, feeling proud.

The flowers dance in a silly sway,
Corrupting bees who forgot their way,
They trip on pollen like it's a game,
The sun laughs too; it's never the same.

Laughter on the Gentle Draft

A soft gust whispers secrets untold,
Rolling past old sheep, brave yet bold,
They tumble down, a fluffy mess,
While the daisies giggle at the stress.

A breeze whooshes through with a tickle and twist,
Leaves join the fun; they simply can't resist,
Listen carefully to the rippling tones,
Nature's silly jokes, just soft undertones.

Harmonies of Nature's Breath

Among the mist, a chorus of glee,
Floating along with a bumblebee,
The clouds roll out their fluffy jokes,
While gophers break dance, my oh my folks!

Tickling tall grass, it all starts to sway,
Frogs ribbit in rhythm, hoot hooray!
No worries in sight, just giggles and cheer,
In this wild concert, we all hold dear.

Soft Murmurs of the Heavens

Low whispers of joy bounce off the rocks,
Tickling the toes of unsuspecting flocks,
The sun throws a pun, the stars crack a smile,
While chipmunks argue who danced the best style.

Clouds conspire with gusts of sweet air,
Planting tickles of giggles everywhere,
On this great stage with actors unseen,
Each chuckle floats by, utterly serene.

Daydreams on the Summer Air

A squirrel wearing shades, what a sight,
He dances on branches, feeling so light.
The sun tickles grass, a warm prank,
While flowers giggle along the riverbank.

A cat on a roof, thinks he's a king,
Swatting at clouds, ready to sing.
Butterflies chatter, gossip they share,
About the odd shape of my messy hair.

Budding Life in Enchanted Gales

Buds burst forth, like popcorn in fun,
Plants throwing a party for everyone.
Bees don tiny hats, buzzing with glee,
As they plan their grand picnic by the old tree.

A worm cracks jokes while the daisies sway,
Telling tales of the earth from their homey stay.
They laugh at the snail, so slow on his quest,
While ants form a line for an unending fest.

Echoing Lullabies Among the Trees

The wind sings softly, a playful tune,
While a raccoon hums to the light of the moon.
Squirrels join in with a clumsy beat,
Creating a symphony that's really quite sweet.

A frog leaps forth, join the show,
Croaking a rhythm he really does know.
Trees sway along, they can't help but sway,
In this wacky concert, they all find a way.

Dreams Unfurled on Silken Breezes

Puppies chasing tails with wild delight,
While butterflies giggle, taking to flight.
Clouds play tag, drifting through the air,
It's a circus of joy, no sign of despair.

A hare tells jokes, in a voice quite grand,
While a tortoise nods, he's a big fan.
They race through the fields, what a scenic chase,
In this dreamy realm, it's all about grace.

Imaginations in Subtle Whispers

A breeze tickles my nose,
I laugh through flowered rows.
The lilies start to dance,
As I'm caught in a trance.

Butterflies wear tiny hats,
While squirrels try on spats.
The clouds are in a race,
What a silly, silly place!

A bird hums a jazzy tune,
Presents a show by the moon.
I join with a wobbly jig,
And hope I don't fall big!

With whispers that tease and play,
The world turns bright and gay.
In this wonderland I find,
Laughter links us all, combined.

A Symphony of Gentle Currents

The leaves sway in a chair,
Breeze tickles without a care.
A frog jumps, slips on a bee,
Creating a ruckus with glee!

Fish flash by with a grin,
In the stream, it's a win-win.
They splash like little clowns,
While I wear my soggy frowns.

Parrots gossip in the trees,
Chattering about the bees.
With a wink and a nod,
I join this lively squad.

The sun dips down and winks,
While laughter floats and sinks.
In this orchestra of fun,
Every note is a bright pun!

Glimpses of Celestial Tranquility

Stars play hide and seek at night,
Winking slowly, what a sight!
Planets spin in cosmic cheer,
With giggles that we all can hear.

A comet zips by, what a thrill,
Like a kid on a wild hill.
Whispers float on galaxy streams,
Tickling all our silliest dreams.

Moonbeams wear pajamas white,
And dance around with sheer delight.
In this absurd cosmic game,
Even the sun rivals their fame.

Such wonders fill the skies,
With laughter and surprise.
Each twinkling little star,
Holds a joke from afar!

Whispers of Serene Winds

The air is a cheeky sprite,
Playing tricks, what a delight!
Pine trees share peculiar tales,
Of chilly gales and happy trails.

A sand crab wears sunglasses bold,
Almost regal, or so I'm told.
With a hop and a shimmy dance,
He recruits me, a happy chance.

Kites flutter, doing pirouettes,
While giggling kids pay their debts.
In between bursts of fresh air,
There's laughter floating everywhere.

With whispers soft and low,
We give in to the flow.
In this breezy, wacky frame,
Every moment's fair game!

Whispers of Serene Winds

Soft whispers float around,
Telling tales of playful clowns.
They tickle trees and dance with glee,
Making the flowers laugh with free.

A squirrel jumps in sheer delight,
As gusts give him a little fright.
He puffs his cheeks, then takes his stand,
While breezes swirl like jesters grand.

Everyone laughs in the sunny air,
As winds play pranks without a care.
They tickle noses and ruffle hair,
Creating chaos everywhere.

And so we sit and giggle loud,
While flies form lines, a comical crowd.
In nature's playground, full of cheer,
Silly winds are what we revere.

Caress of a Sunlit Zephyr

Zephyrs tease the flowers bright,
Whispering secrets, oh what a sight!
They flirt with petals, prance and play,
Turning blooms into a cabaret.

A bee buzzes, feeling suave,
As breezes give him a little shove.
He flips and flops in floral bliss,
Seduced by sunlight in every kiss.

The grass joins in, it sways like mad,
Creating rhythms, oh so glad.
With each caress, they spin around,
What a dance, with laughter crowned!

We take a moment, breathe it in,
The air is filled with giggles and grins.
A light prank here, a twist of fate,
In this free-for-all, we celebrate!

Sighs of Celestial Currents

High above, the currents sigh,
With flirty winds that tease the sky.
They play tag with a fluffy cloud,
And laugh aloud, so very proud.

A bird takes flight, then spins with grace,
Chasing breezes in a wild race.
He squawks in glee, "Catch me if you can!"
As winds turn cheeky and make their plan.

Laughter drifts through the evening glow,
As twirling leaves put on a show.
Each gust a giggle, each swirl a jest,
In nature's humor, we find our rest.

So here's to whirls and whimsical sighs,
To playful currents that never lie.
With every breeze, we celebrate,
Life's grand humor is truly great!

Embrace of Ethereal Winds

Winds embrace with a gentle tease,
As nature dances with perfect ease.
They swirl around, a playful crew,
Making mischief as they blew.

The bushes shake, they're in a spin,
While critters laugh, they join in.
A hedgehog wiggles, a laugh so loud,
In windswept chaos, feels quite proud.

The trees tell jokes, their leaves a-shake,
While giggling with every little quake.
Sunshine beamed with cheeky flair,
As breezy banter filled the air.

So let's enjoy this windy jest,
Where laughter flows, we feel so blessed.
In every gust, we find delight,
In nature's humor, hearts take flight!

Rhapsody of Flora's Gentle Touch

Pollen's a prankster, tickling your nose,
As daisies and daisies strike playful poses.
Giggling tulips sway, they know they're the best,
In a garden fiesta, they never rest!

Butterflies chuckle, with each silly dance,
While the roses gossip, giving love a chance.
Petals do somersaults, sprightly and bright,
In the fiesta of blooms, everything feels right!

A Canvas of Feathered Zephyrs

Birds in a row, they wear tiny hats,
Singing in chorus, oh, what cheeky brats!
Feathers a-flutter, making quite a scene,
They trade all their jokes, you know what I mean?

With a wiggle and giggle, they perch on a wire,
Planning their mischief, they never retire.
A dance-off ensues, wings flapping in cheer,
Watch out, goofy sprits, wishes abound here!

Summertime Lull in Paradise Lost

Oh, the ice cream truck is a musical dream,
With a jingle that flows like a sunbeam's gleam.
Each cone is a treasure, oh, what a delight,
As sprinkles rain down, everything feels right!

Sunshine is giggling, through a glass of soda,
And ants with tiny hats say, 'Can we join the quota?'
As laughter erupts at the park full of fun,
Every moment is golden, bathing in sun!

The Secret Life of Silent Winds

Whispers of laughter flit past your ear,
As secrets get carried from faraway spheres.
A tickle from nowhere runs up your spine,
Plays hide-and-seek, oh, how divine!

Kites pulled with giggles sway high in the sky,
The breeze tells tall tales of a pie in a spy.
Serenity masks a ruckus in flight,
In the stillness you feel, the play's pure delight!

Ethereal Currents in Bloom

A gust that tickles, oh so sly,
It whispers jokes as it zips by.
Leaves giggle high, branches sway,
Nature's banter, come out and play!

Dandelions dance, their seeds take flight,
In this wild waltz, they twirl with delight.
A butterfly's laugh makes flowers blush,
In this breezy romp, there's never a rush.

Clouds pass by with a cheeky grin,
Raindrops drop jokes with a splash and spin.
The humor of nature sings loud and clear,
With every soft rustle, you've got to hear!

In the orchard, the wind sways a tease,
Fruits fall down with a comical ease.
Lemons roll, and apples tumble too,
In this joyful breeze, the laughter's for you!

Shimmers of Nature's Breath

A whispering gale with a playful twist,
Turns frowns upside down, it can't be missed.
As daisies chuckle, the daisies seem wise,
Tickling your nose, a trick in disguise.

Squirrels chatter, their tails in a fuss,
As the wind carries tales on a rustling bus.
What's that I hear? A cotton candy cloud,
Bristling with giggles, oh so loud!

The feathery touch of a wise old tree,
Is just nature saying, "Hey, come play with me!"
In this breath of delight, joy's in the air,
And even the crickets start a dance with flair.

A breeze so funny, it trips with a wink,
While flowers laugh secret jokes, don't you think?
So wear a smile, let your worries be few,
For laughter blossoms in all that we do!

Harmony in a Sunlit Whisper

Breezy banter in the afternoon light,
Shadows of chuckles take playful flight.
Flowers lean in, ears open wide,
For gossip of sunshine and giggles, they hide.

Sailing the air like a kite made of cheer,
A tickle of breeze, "Hey, have you heard here!"
Ducks quack at plans to have picnic galore,
While bees hum along, "Oh, let's get some more!"

Whispers swirl like ice cream on cones,
Flavors of fun melt into silly tones.
A gust full of jokes, a sweet little jest,
Brings kindness in laughter, it's truly the best.

On pathways bright, where kids run and play,
The wind gives them secrets, "Let's have a say!"
With laughter and warmth, the world becomes bright,
In whispers of joy, everything feels right.

Cascading Air Over Blossoms

A whirlwind of chuckles overhead,
With petals and puffs, where do they spread?
Breezes conspire with jokes from afar,
While blossoms laugh back—what a bizarre char!

In gardens they mingle, the butterflies cheer,
As the wind tells them tales, "You've nothing to fear!"
A leaf lightly flutters, it beckons the rain,
"Oh dear, I might slip—what's that? Am I sane?"

The pollen is partying, a sneeze just for fun,
"Watch where it blows; oh, the antics have begun!"
Sweet scents of mischief drape through the air,
As the flowers join in, without a single care.

Even the tulips join in the spree,
Wiggling their stems, they spring with glee.
A chorus of laughter, their petals shimmer bright,
In the breezy ballet, everything feels right!

Float of the Ambrosial Wind

A feather floats by on a whim,
It dances with joy, no need to swim.
A squirrel giggles as it runs,
Chasing the breeze, oh what fun!

The shadows tickle the grassy floor,
As bees are busy, they start to roar.
A snail slips past, looking quite smug,
While butterflies prance, cozy and snug.

The sun shines bright with a cheeky grin,
While daisies chuckle, oh where to begin?
Laughter echoes through leafy trees,
As critters play tag, riding the breeze.

A whirlwind of joy, it can't be tamed,
Nature's party, nobody named.
Come join the fun, leave worries behind,
In this wondrous chaos, all joyfully aligned.

Glistening Tides of a Gentle Gale

Waves swirl in a giggling spree,
As seagulls squawk, all wild and free.
The fish flip-flop to join the song,
While crabs keep dancing, don't get me wrong.

The sun dips down, a golden snack,
As jellyfish jiggle, not looking back.
A tumbleweed rolls, with no sense of care,
While whales send jokes through the salty air.

The tide pulls back like a giant prank,
Tickling toes, what a messy rank!
Seaweed wiggles, looking quite slick,
As dolphins dive in, quick and quick.

When the moon takes a peek, it laughs out loud,
While clam shells chatter, feeling so proud.
The ocean's a circus, waves in a twirl,
Where laughter's the treasure, come take a whirl!

A Song of Nature's Embrace

In the meadow, frogs croak a tune,
While clouds float by, a fluffy platoon.
A rabbit hops, with such bouncy flair,
Waving at flowers, without a care.

The trees wear whispers, secrets to share,
As the wind spins tales, twisting in air.
Ants plan a picnic under the sun,
Stealing crumbs, oh it's all in good fun!

A chubby bear waves, wearing a hat,
While chipmunks giggle, going pitter-pat.
A kite fills the sky, as kids run around,
Chasing their giggles, never to drown.

Nature hums softly, a melody sweet,
Creating a rhythm, with a funny beat.
Join in the chorus, let laughter ignite,
In the embrace of the day, everything's right.

Echoes of the World's Exhale

The hills yawn wide, stretching with glee,
As valleys whisper secrets, just for me.
A raccoon rolls over, playing so bold,
While shadows dance lightly, warming the cold.

The rivers chuckle, making a splash,
As rocks play hopscotch, what a big bash!
A goose in shades strikes a pose so nice,
While turtles chuckle, oh isn't it dice?

The clouds trade jests, a glittery show,
As thistles spin tales from long ago.
The wind winks slyly, what a good tease,
While sunbeams tumble through rustling leaves.

The world's a stage, so laugh and play,
As nature's orchestra joins the ballet.
Join the echoes, feel the fun swell,
In this joyous realm where laughter does dwell.

Floating on a Sigh of Delight

Up in the sky, where kites take flight,
A tickle of winds brings laughs, so light.
Chasing my hair like a playful cat,
I swat at the air, wondering where it's at.

Socks on the line, they dance with glee,
Twisting and turning, a funny spree.
Wind says 'hello' with a cheeky grin,
And I reply, 'where have you been?'

Ice cream in hand, it starts to drip,
The breeze steals a scoop, oh what a trip!
Running to catch it, feet in a race,
The sun starts to chuckle, a warm embrace.

Even the trees are laughing today,
Branches swing low as if they want to play.
So here's to the air, the joy it brings,
Whirling in laughter while eternity sings.

Tracery of Celestial Breezes

Whispers of gusts hug my side,
Tickling my ears, oh what a ride!
Jackets and hats become wayward fools,
Dancing around like they play by the rules.

Balloons take flight, not a care in sight,
One snags a cloud, what a comical fright!
The sun winks down, it knows the game,
As squirrels look up, it's all quite the shame.

Laughing daisies sway, oh what a sight,
Bouncing around in the shimmering light.
They tell me a joke, but I can't keep pace,
With petals aflutter, it's a wild chase.

As night falls, the moon starts to play,
With breezes that whisper secrets every way.
So float on the laughter, ride each delight,
With whims of the wind, it's a humorous flight.

Suspension in the Garden's Breath

In the garden of giggles, the daisies cheer,
Whispering secrets to all who wander near.
A bee with a buzz, like a joke, it flies,
Tripping through flowers, oh what a surprise!

The tomatoes blush, they just can't believe,
Why cucumbers wear shades, oh who would conceive?
Lettuce gets jealous, "Why can't I be cool?"
While spinach just nods, "We're all in this school."

The breeze lifts confetti from sylvan delight,
Turning the flowers into a colorful sight.
Frogs at the pond chuckle, what a party,
While ants march in line, looking quite hearty.

Dandelions puff tales of whimsical lore,
As tall tales float up and then tumble to shore.
So let's toss our worries, let the laughter fly,
In this garden of joy, where jokes never die.

Delight in the Patience of Airflows

Sailboats in puddles on a breezy day,
Rippling with laughter, oh what a display!
The wind shows off in a charming parade,
While puddles take turns, a silly charade.

Chasing the sun, I skip down the lane,
Every gust teasing with a playful refrain.
Cows in the field laugh with the breeze,
Mooing their jokes, trying hard to please.

A kite soars high, with a tale to share,
It tickles the clouds, no worries or cares.
Each twist and turn, it conquers the blue,
With giggles and chuckles, it dances on cue.

So let's raise our voices to the tickling air,
In the laughter-filled sky, we've nothing to spare.
With breezy delights that sway near and far,
We'll meet each fresh gust, like a shooting star.

Sun-kissed Currents of Bliss

Gold rays tickle the skin,
A seagull steals my fries,
Laughter mingles with waves,
As the beach ball flies high.

Sandy toes dance in the sun,
And sunscreen smells like cheer,
A toddler trips and has fun,
Splashing water everywhere near.

Ice cream drips down my hand,
A sunburned nose grins bright,
Flip-flops both on the wrong feet,
This is summer's pure delight.

With every breeze, I chuckle,
Nature's wit brings a tease,
Life's a beach, and I'm wobbly,
Riding laughter like the sea's ease.

Petals in the Air

Flower confetti flies high,
As bees chase butterflies,
A sneeze makes flowers scatter,
Like nature's sweet surprise.

A squirrel steals my sandwich,
While I laugh and shout,
Petals twirl in the wind,
As if they're dancing about.

Sneaky snails on a mission,
Slow dancing on the grass,
A petulant pup joins in,
Chasing petals as they pass.

The garden's an uproar,
With chaos everywhere,
Yet in that wild laughter,
Bliss seems to float in the air.

Whirling Leaves of Autumn

Leaves swirl down like confetti,
As I trip on one too slick,
Laughter echoes all around,
In the park, it's quite the trick.

A pumpkin rolls from a cart,
As kids squeal with delight,
Autumn's fun is all a part,
Of this seasonal light fight.

Crunchy snacks under foot,
A squirrel surveys the scene,
Suddenly he makes a move,
And in my lap, he's seen!

Cozy sweaters wrapped round,
Hot cocoa spills on my shoe,
In this season of giggles,
Even mishaps feel brand new.

Solace in the Gentle Drift

Clouds parade in the sky,
As I lounge in a chair,
A gentle drift of calmness,
Makes me forget my cares.

Sunflowers nod with laughter,
As bees buzz their way through,
Butterflies mock my stretching,
Oh, what a silly view!

A hammock swings lightly low,
While I sip lemonade,
An awkward cat joins the show,
And my joy can't be delayed.

Whispers of soft joy linger,
While the breeze hums a tune,
In this cozy little spot,
Life feels like a fun cartoon.

Raindrops and Laughing Winds

Raindrops dance on my nose,
Tickling my toes as they pose.
A squirrel sneezes, it's quite the sight,
Chasing its tail in pure delight.

Puddles reflect the goofy glee,
As frogs croak out a symphony.
With each gust, the giggles soar,
Who knew the sky could be a chore?

The clouds wear hats, and what a show,
Blowing kisses with each blow.
As I leap, I trip, and then I grin,
Wondering if laughter's a sin.

A rainbow slides down the sun's back,
A silly dance, a color attack.
In this wild weather, I'm feeling wise,
That laughter's gold, and it's no surprise!

Flickers of Light Through the Breeze

Sunbeams peek through leafy green,
Whispering secrets, oh so keen.
A beetle twirls, it's quite the twist,
Where are the dancers? They've all missed!

The wind wears sneakers with loud designs,
Bounding 'round like fun-loving rhymes.
As shadows jiggle, the sun starts to wink,
Who knew the air could make us think?

Butterflies stumble in mid-air flights,
They've mistaken leaves for stage lights.
Flickers of joy, they flutter with flair,
What a wacky world we all share!

A monochrome cat joins the tune,
Chasing sunbeams like a cartoon.
Nature's humor, it's never stale,
In this festival, we shall prevail!

An Invitation from the Air

The whispers of leaves sway in delight,
Inviting all critters to the night.
A raccoon prances, showing off shoes,
With every step, it shares the news!

Crisp breezes ruffle a picnic spread,
While ants parade, forming a thread.
They feast on crumbs like kings of the grass,
Making me wonder how long they'll last.

Fireflies flash like lost disco balls,
Offering the night some funny calls.
While shadows giggle under the moon,
An air of laughter makes hearts swoon.

Join the jesters of leaf and light,
Where every twirl sparks pure delight.
With nature's charm in every breeze,
We dance through life with silly ease!

Secrets Carried by Soft Air

Soft whispers tickle the tops of trees,
Sharing tall tales with playful ease.
A chipmunk shrugs, 'tis just a breeze,'
While I trip over my own two knees.

The wind carries gossip of birds and bees,
While ants in tuxedos command their fees.
A squirrel debates, 'Should I try for flight?'
Jumping so high, it lands with fright!

Puffy clouds plot, with mischief in mind,
Gamifying raindrops, so blissfully blind.
Each droplet giggles, as it splatters down,
Creating a symphony, wearing a crown.

Nature's chuckle, a soft serenade,
Reminds us all, life's best masquerade.
So take a breath in this airy delight,
And join the laughter that fills the night!

Driftwood in the Heart of Summer

On sandy shores, we build our dreams,
A crab scuttles by, or so it seems.
"With sunburned backs, we laugh and shout,
Who knew the ocean could flop about?"

With ice cream cones that melt away,
We chase the waves and try to play.
"Hey, look! A fish!" one kid will scream,
While others ponder life's grand scheme.

In flip-flops lost, we march in line,
The lifeguard's gaze—not quite divine.
"Next summer's plan: a yacht, not this!"
We toss our hats with ocean bliss.

A seagull swoops down for a bite,
"Hey! That's my lunch!"—a comical sight.
We laugh as it flies, a thief in flight,
Under the sun, our spirits are bright!

Colors of the Whispering Sky

The clouds are dancing, what a show!
They twist and twirl, like kids we know.
"Look! That one's a cat!" a voice will sound,
As we lie on the grass, feet off the ground.

The sun paints rainbows, oh so sly,
While bugs debate on how to fly.
"Do grasshoppers hop? Or are they just shy?"
We giggle at thoughts that flutter by.

A breezy joke, the leaves they share,
"Why'd the tree stop? It had no hair!"
With giggles echoing skyward light,
We ponder what else is truly bright.

A kite gets tangled, oh what a plight,
"It's part of the show!" we joke in delight.
Among the colors, we find our glee,
In the whispering sky, we feel so free.

Midsummer's Gentle Caress

A parade of ants marches by my shoe,
"Hey, where's the party? Invite us too!"
With lemonade sips and laughter's charm,
We swat away heat with no alarm.

The sun beams bright, a fickle friend,
"Don't roast too long, we still pretend!"
With shady spots, we take our stand,
And build a fort of grass and sand.

A lizard stares with curious eyes,
"Are we the giants?" it seems to surmise.
We roll around, make silly faces,
While time slips by in these funny places.

When evening comes, the stars will peek,
"Can one small star outshine the cheek?"
We chuckle loud, a midsummer's jest,
In this gentle warmth, we are so blessed!

The Dance of Fainting Shadows

Flickering shadows leap and play,
As daylight starts to fade away.
"Is that a ghost? Or just some fun?"
We laugh as the dance has just begun.

The lamp post wobbles, what a sight,
"It's doing the cha-cha!"—we hold on tight.
With giggles rising as night draws near,
We tease the dark, banishing fear.

A mouse peeks out, thinking it sly,
"Is this a shadow? Do I spy?"
We chuckle soft at its tiny plight,
While whispering tales of a flying kite.

So here we gather, friends so dear,
In dancing shadows, we have no fear.
With laughter soaring, joy spreads wide,
In this playful world, we always abide!

Songs in the Woven Leaves

In the dance of trees above,
The leaves sing tunes of love.
A squirrel jumps, a branch does sway,
I trip on roots, but hey, hooray!

The sun peeks in with golden rays,
Tickling my nose, a game it plays.
I chase the wind, it tickles me,
Giggles escape, wild and free!

A butterfly wears silly socks,
Buzzing bees in comical flocks.
An acorn rolls, a race begins,
Nature laughs, oh what fun spins!

The flowers sway in a silly row,
They whisper jokes, don't you know?
With every gust, they curl and lean,
Unruly giggles in the green!

Surrender to the Calm Drift

On a floating leaf, I sit and sway,
A tiny frog croaks, 'Join the play!'
The waters giggle, ripple and dance,
I curse my luck, no time to prance.

A raft of ducks, all in a line,
Each quack a joke, just divine.
I wave my hands, they start to quack,
'Take your time, there's no way back!'

The clouds parade in silly hats,
Chasing shadows, avoiding chats.
Fish splash, they're in on the game,
Who knew the pond was quite the fame?

As I lay back, the world does spin,
With laughter wrapped, I'm pulled right in.
The sun shouts jokes from up above,
In this drift, I find my love!

Flight of Wishes on the Air

Paper planes soar, take a dive,
Each one dreams it's alive!
They zig and zag through cotton fluff,
'No turbulence, this isn't tough!'

A bird pops in with a caw and cheer,
'What's that smell? Is it snack time here?'
I toss some crumbs, but they grow tired,
A laugh erupts, the snack backfired!

A kite in the sky, with a grin so wide,
Teasing the clouds, with a joyous glide.
It sneezes out rainbows, wild and bright,
Giving the sun a ticklish fright!

The wind whispers softly, a playful tease,
It tugs at my hair, it's never please.
With every wish, I let them fly,
In this madness, I learn to cry!

Floating Beyond with Each Breath

Inhale the warmth, exhale the cheer,
The butterflies dance, never fear!
Each breath a giggle, a puff of fun,
Chasing the sunlight, I'm on the run!

Clouds puffed high like marshmallow fluff,
I take a leap, but whoa, that's tough!
They bounce and tease, so soft and light,
I land on grass, oh what a sight!

Here come the daisies, cracking wise,
A sunflower winks, gives me surprise.
They whisper, 'Stay, we'll share some jokes!'
I laugh so hard, I shake like folks!

Floating through laughter, I skip and spin,
With every chuckle, I'm bound to win.
This paradise, it pulls me in tight,
With humor and joy, my heart takes flight!

Souvenirs of Wind and Light

A feather danced from tree to tree,
I wondered if it wanted to flee.
It whispered jokes unheard by the sun,
As squirrels played tag, just for fun.

A gust swirled leaves like a dancer's skirt,
While ducks quacked loudly, 'We're not hurt!'
The shadows giggled, casting a prank,
As rabbits dressed up for a formal rank.

Breezes carried scents of fresh-baked pies,
While ants held a meeting beneath blue skies.
They plotted a feast, a tiny buffet,
While above, a kite soared, making hay.

Oh, the memories made by the air so light,
Turning ordinary days into sheer delight.
With each soft rustle and every twirl,
Nature's comedians share a cheeky whirl.

Twilight's Cool Embrace

As twilight draped the world in gray,
A cat decided to start ballet.
The branches clapped, the stars were loud,
While fireflies waltzed, oh what a crowd!

A breeze came in, all dressed in blue,
Tickling the leaves with a giggly brew.
The night critters gathered for a chat,
While frogs crooned love songs, wouldn't you bet?

Moonlight mischief brushed over the field,
Where crickets played ciphers, they refused to yield.
A squirrel piped up, "I'll crack a nut!"
As nearby a hedgehog acted all strut.

In the midst of whispers and laughter's thrill,
The dusk held secrets, an endless spill.
With each whispering sound, night wore a grin,
In twilight's embrace, the fun would begin.

Spirit Rides on the Wind

A gust chased a kite with joyful flair,
While spirits rode high without a care.
The daisies chuckled and swayed with ease,
As whispers of wisdom fluttered like bees.

The clouds played peek-a-boo with the moon,
While echoes of laughter filled the afternoon.
A squirrel in aviator goggles flew,
Shouting, "Hold tight! I'll take you too!"

The breeze hummed tunes, a soft serenade,
Where shadows and colors cheekily played.
Leaves shared gossip, fluttering in fun,
As ants in two-step out danced everyone.

In these moments of folly, the air came alive,
Where the spirit of laughter would always thrive.
A carousel of moments, sweet and bright,
Whirling with joy in the softening light.

Notes of Solitude in Surging Air

In quiet corners, the breeze mocks the still,
As leaves scribble notes, their movement a thrill.
With each tiny rustle, secrets unfold,
A symphony of giggles from stories untold.

A porcupine ponders, lost in thought,
While wispy tendrils swirl, his troubles forgot.
The wind whispered jokes of the clouds up high,
As chirping birds laughed from the nearby sky.

Cactuses chuckled in the desert's embrace,
While shadows danced around, keeping pace.
In every breeze was mischief and cheer,
A reminder that laughter is always near.

So when solitude's hand plays a cheeky tune,
Let the whispers of air make your heart swoon.
For life is a jest, with joy to share,
In the world where notes of laughter fill the air.

Cradled Moments in Soft Air

In the shade of a dancing tree,
Monkeys swing with glee,
Chasing their tails around,
While I laugh at the sound.

A bird drops a snack on my head,
I pretend it's not happening, instead,
The squirrels giggle as they peek,
"Who's the clumsy one? Oh, the tweak!"

With laughter filling the space,
I join a race with a turtle's pace,
He grins with a cheeky flair,
"Fast and slow? Who really cares?"

As the sun begins to wane,
I'm caught in a froggy refrain,
Croaks mix with my chuckle-plight,
Here's to joy in the soft twilight!

Cascade of Windy Promises

A kite dances low, then high,
It swirls like it's trying to fly,
But tangled in a bush, it stays,
While I laugh at its windy delays.

A gust gives my hat a flip,
I chase it on a silly trip,
With each step, I take a slide,
My shoes join in the windy ride.

Leaves flutter like they're in a rush,
While I stumble in a leafy hush,
The trees chuckle, waving their arms,
At the mess of my clumsy charms.

When evening falls, the winds chat low,
I whisper secrets to them, you know,
A promise made, a giggle shared,
In this hilarious breeze, we're ensnared!

Vows on a Festive Breeze

A parade of balloons in the air,
Promising joy without a care,
One escapes with a cheeky whine,
"I'm off to find my own sunshine!"

Confetti drifts, a colorful scene,
While a puppy leaps, all so keen,
To catch what dances in the sky,
As I laugh at his woeful try.

Bells jingle, and laughter swirls,
I twirl in delight, like a girl,
Forget the dance, let's just prance,
In a shindig of silly chance!

As vows of mirth fill the day's end,
I wish you could hold my hand, friend,
For in this air of giggly glee,
Together we'd dance, wild and free!

A Journey through Invisible Currents

On a raft of giggles, we drift,
Riding waves of a playful lift,
A fish sneaks up with a wink,
"I'd trade my hook for a drink!"

The current chuckles, swirls around,
It tickles our toes on the ground,
A sea turtle joins, with a grin,
"Want a ride, or just to spin?"

With every splash, we laugh and dive,
In this watery dance, we're alive,
The bubbles rise; they pop and play,
A milky way in a fun-filled spray!

As the currents guide our delight,
We sail into the starry night,
In this ocean of jocular trails,
We find humor as our wind-filled sails!

Celestial Drafts of Reverie

A tickle from the leaves above,
Whispers like a playful dove.
Chasing squirrels who are quite sly,
As popcorn clouds drift in the sky.

Laughter rides on the twilight breeze,
Dancing shadows, shimmying trees.
A butterfly flaunts its vibrant style,
While dragonflies giggle all the while.

In this paradise, who needs a seat?
The grass is soft, it makes life sweet.
Banana peels toss and curl,
As ants plan their mission to whirl.

Roaming rabbits with cheeky grins,
Telling tales of their odd wins.
Wiggling their noses with glee and flair,
This is the life, without a care.

Hushed Murmurs of Awakened Flora

Flowers gossip in colors bright,
Discussing petals under the moonlight.
Daisies chuckle in the morning sun,
While daisies wink, 'Life is fun!'

The tulips prance in a silly dance,
Creating laughter with every chance.
A sunflower jokes about its height,
Claiming it's the star of the night.

Vines twist and curl like a playful cat,
Tickling bees who are all about that.
Pollen particles join in the chat,
While ladybugs tease with a light pat.

Fragrant breezes stir up delight,
In this garden, everything's bright.
Each petal a story, each leaf a song,
Where even the weeds get along!

Breath of a Gilded Dawn

The sun breaks with a stunning cheer,
Chasing away the night's old fear.
Roosters crowing, 'Rise and shine!'
While cats stretch like they just crossed a line.

A giggle runs through the waking town,
As morning joggers wear a frown.
Coffee scents tickle the air so sweet,
While squirrels dance with little feet.

Waves of laughter crash like the tide,
As breakfast toast takes a funny ride.
Butterflies sashay with grace and flair,
Spreading joy like they just don't care.

Sunshine tickles the sleepy grass,
Promising fun as moments pass.
With every glow, the world ignites,
In the golden light, everything excites.

Secrets of the Serene Horizon

Waves of mischief lap at the shore,
Where whispers of laughter forever soar.
Seagulls squawk in their silly way,
Making up stories to brighten the day.

Horizons stretch like candy canes,
With colors vibrant, breaking the chains.
Every sunset is a grand parade,
As shadows dance in the cool glade.

Pine trees sway with a gentle tease,
Sharing secrets carried by the breeze.
A lighthouse giggles, tipping its hat,
Winking at boats, now how 'bout that?

On cliffs of joy, where laughter's born,
Frolicking waves just can't be worn.
Frogs wear crowns, thinking they're kings,
Unraveling the joy that nature brings.

A Symphony of Whispering Leaves

In the trees where gossip flows,
Leaves crack jokes and everyone knows.
Squirrels giggle, oh what a scene,
As they plot with each shiny bean.

The branches sway with playful cheer,
Tickling noses as they draw near.
A rustle here, a chuckle there,
Nature's laughter fills the air.

With a flip and flap, the birds take flight,
They love to tease, oh what a sight!
With a wink and a nod, they spread their wings,
Whispering secrets of strange little things.

In this green kingdom of funny delight,
Where shadows dance and joy takes flight.
The whispers echo, the laughter swells,
As nature chirps her merry bells.

Dancing Wisp of Moonlit Nights

Under the moon with a mischievous grin,
A wisp of laughter, let the fun begin.
Fireflies jiggle, they dance and twirl,
As the night spins out in a twinkly whirl.

The stars giggle, tickling the sky,
While owls hoot, and crickets comply.
A frog leaps high, aiming for fame,
In this silly game, it jumps again with no shame.

Each shadow plays, a trickster's delight,
Casting goofy shapes in the pale moonlight.
With a swipe of a tail, a raccoon appears,
Stealing snacks, while chortling cheers.

Oh, what a night of frolic and fun,
When the moon's on your side, mischief's never done.
So dance, little wisp, with a bounce and a flair,
For in this night, joy fills the air.

The Elysian Serenade of Air

A gentle tune wafts through the trees,
Where giggles linger like a sweet breeze.
Mice in bow ties start to prance,
Frolicking joyfully in a silly dance.

Clouds fluff up, like popcorn bright,
As dandelions twirl in pure delight.
The sun winks down, a cheeky face,
Inviting laughter to take its place.

What a concert of chirps and squeaks,
Where even the shyest critter peeks.
With a rap and a tap, they jam all day,
Creating laughter, come what may.

Oh, the things that float in the air,
All the giggles and little dares.
In this joyful realm, where spirits lifting,
Every breath is a gift, this world is gifting.

Essence of the Enchanted Grove

Deep in the woods, where laughter blooms,
Chasing shadows, dispelling glooms.
A raccoon's hat's askew and bright,
As he plots a prank under the moonlight.

With ticklish grass where fairies bound,
They spin and whirl, they leap around.
A squirrel's trumpet announces the jest,
Calling all friends for a whimsy fest.

The trees whisper of secrets so bold,
As hoots and howls begin to unfold.
A treasure hunt leads to silly finds,
Like mismatched socks and fumbled winds.

Where smiles grow wild and worry is few,
Nature's jokes enchant the crew.
In this grove where mirth does thrive,
Every creature dances, joy alive.

Chime of Distant Chimes

In a field where the odd socks roam,
They dance around, far from home.
A hat's on a cow, a fence is askew,
And laughter's the language, it knows how to woo.

With a breeze like a barber, it swoops and it sways,
It tickles the daisies and gives them some rays.
The crickets in tuxedos start tap dancing loud,
While the turtles play checkers, both fancy and proud.

Clouds wear sunglasses and lounge in the sky,
Pigs fly on jetpacks, oh me, oh my!
In this realm of zany, where odd is the norm,
Every gust is a giggle, a fanciful charm.

So come take a seat on a comical chair,
Watch rabbits in waistcoats jog without a care.
In the whistle and chime, where the laughter aligns,
Even the sun wears a grin, and that's how it shines.

Breezes that Paint the Horizon

When the air takes a brush with a wink from the sun,
It colors the daisies, all yellow and fun.
A squirrel sports a beret, looking quite chic,
As the wind hums a tune, oh so unique.

With a twist and a twirl, the leaves start to prance,
They form a conga line, inviting a dance.
A raccoon in a tutu attempts to ballet,
While the clouds chuckle softly, "Today's our play day!"

A gust of fresh humor flutters by, oh so sly,
It tickles the noses of those passing by.
The grass grows a giggle, the flowers all laugh,
As butterflies practice their best autograph.

So let's chase the colors, let's run with the breeze,
Join the waltz of the charming, where laughter's the tease.
From paintbrush to laughter, let joy be our call,
In this whimsical world, come one, come all!

Mirages Born on Gentle Air

A mirage made of jellybeans dances in sight,
While unicorns juggle with rainbows so bright.
The whispers of whispers float soft in our ears,
And the trees trade their secrets while sipping cold beers.

With each gentle zephyr, a joke drifts along,
A big toe-shaped cloud bursts into a song.
The mountains wear hats like a wise old grandpa,
While the river just giggles, "Ain't this a fun saga?"

The sun throws a party, inviting the moon,
They boogie with stars to an old-timey tune.
With funny parades, where the laughter runs free,
The world spins in circles, just wait and you'll see.

So follow the mirage, it's more than it seems,
In this whimsical land, full of silly dreams.
For laughter is magic, as air can affirm,
Join the jest of the world, let your heart be the term.

Spirits of the Autumn Wind

When leaves lightly tumble like feathers in flight,
They gossip with giggles and dance without fright.
A scarecrow with shades sways on his tall post,
To the beat of the laughter, he's dancing the most.

With whispers of chill, and a pinch of good cheer,
The pumpkins tell stories we're eager to hear.
And the owls in their spectacles borrow a line,
From the breeze as it chuckles, "Now this is divine!"

The nuts play a game, 'Who can roll down the hill?'
While the whispers of autumn give laughter a thrill.
A fox with a top hat does cartwheels with ease,
While the pumpkins break out into fits of a tease.

So let's cherish the breezes that carry our glee,
In a festival of folly, where we're all wild and free.
For in each gust of sweetness, we find our delight,
With spirits of laughter, we party all night!

Dance of the Leisurely Gales

Whispers play hide and seek,
As squirrels attempt a silly streak.
Leaves toss in a giggly swish,
Even branches start to wish.

Dandelions laugh in the breeze,
Tickled by wandering amateur wees.
Stars twinkle, does that mean a show?
That one tree is dancing, don't you know?

Grass does a shimmy, what a sight!
The sun winks, laughing at the night.
June bugs cha-cha on the path,
Not taking life too serious, for laughs!

With a cool touch that brings delight,
Nature's joke invites the night.
In the air, a secret lies,
Is giggling grass the ultimate prize?

Breezy Serenades at Dusk

As evening's glow paints the sky,
Gentle gusts tiptoe and sigh.
A cat ducks, then pounces near,
Was that breeze just having a cheer?

Crickets tap dance on the ground,
To the rhythm of laughter they've found.
Moonlight twirls, a silver swirl,
Even shadows join in a whirl.

The breeze throws a party, so sweet,
It's a barbecue for ants, what a treat!
Mosquitoes join in with a sting,
But they're just the clowns of the fling.

Balloons float, chasing the stars,
With a breeze that teases like guitars.
Every creature laughs in the air,
A concert of whimsy, beyond compare!

Chasing Shadows of Fluffy Clouds

Puffy figures drift so high,
Chasing dreams as they pass by.
A sheep in the sky? No way!
Just cotton candy gone astray.

Breezes toss in cheeky grins,
As sunbeams fight, where to begin?
Clouds roll on, don't they know?
They're the comedians of the show!

Kites join the chase, flapping wings,
In this wacky realm, laughter sings.
Whirligigs spin with a cackle,
Breezy antics break the shackles.

Keep your sunglasses on, oh wow!
What a sight, what fun is now!
As dreams drift and laughter flies,
Fluffy clouds hide the best surprise!

Twilight's Embrace in the Air

Twilight whispers soft and sly,
Sending gales that flirt and fly.
Crickets bicker, loud and proud,
Joking loudly to the crowd.

The stars in jest twinkle bright,
While clouds hold secrets of the night.
With a breeze that makes hearts dance,
Everything sways in a funny prance.

Squirrels gossip, tails held high,
As flowers giggle, oh my oh my!
A warm breeze teases a kind wave,
Pretending it's a knight, so brave!

So let's enjoy this joyful air,
With nuts and laughter everywhere.
Twilight croons to the trees that sway,
Dancing in life's grand ballet!

Finding Peace among the Gusts

In the park, a kite took flight,
A dog chased after with all its might.
But oops! It tangled in a tree,
Now it's a cat's new place to be.

Lemonade cups spill on the ground,
As laughter echoes all around.
We run in circles, what a sight!
With ice cream dripped, we take to flight.

Sun hats fly, oh what a scene,
A gusty day, so fresh and keen.
We dance with joy, in silly cheer,
And wave to the clouds, "What brings you here?"

A breeze so light, it's quite absurd,
It lifts our hair, no need for words.
We spin and twirl, what a bold sport,
In this wind buffet, we never fall short.

Freedom Found in Whirling Air

Around we whirl with glee and grace,
Each gust a tickle, a happy chase.
Cupcakes fly, frosting in tow,
I dodge a cream cloud, just to show!

Racing squirrels, they join the fun,
Chasing acorns, oh what a run!
We leap with joy, arms wide and free,
Who knew wild winds bring such glee?

Giggles burst from every side,
As leaves take off, they cannot hide.
We swat the flies, oh what a spree,
In this whirlwind carnival, just you and me!

Hope the weather won't go sour,
We'll dance till sunset, hour by hour.
The air is wild, but so are we,
Together in this gusty jubilee!

Chasing Flickering Hues

Colorful kites paint the sky,
As we leap, oh, we just fly!
Our faces lit with pure delight,
We race the breeze, chasing light.

Gazing up, dodging sunbeams,
Crafting art from laughter and dreams.
Twirling hats, oh dear, they flee!
That sunset's hue just winked at me!

With every gust, our spirits hum,
The world spins bright; we all become.
A wobbly dance, we can't ignore,
As shadows play, we beg for more!

Funny how colors sway and leap,
In this zany chase, who needs sleep?
We'll paint the sky with all our pa-lay,
Laughing in hues that never decay.

To Dance with the Swaying Shadows

The sunlight winks, the shadows prance,
We join them too in this strange dance.
With giggles swirling, quite a sight,
As shadows twist and hold on tight.

Jumping figures, like popcorn popped,
Through swirling winds, we can't be stopped.
Frolicking with the ground so low,
Beneath the sun, we steal the show!

A gusty friend with a tickling hand,
Whispers secrets, oh how grand!
It lifts our hearts, our feet in flight,
As we twirl away, so full of light!

Our laughter dances through the air,
With every sway, a breath of flair.
In this delightful wind-blown jest,
We find our joy, and truly blessed.

Oceans of Communication in the Wind

Whispers tickle leaves up high,
As seagulls squawk and pigeons sigh.
Each gust a laugh, a silly jest,
Who knew the sky could be so blessed?

Clouds gossip pass with lots of flair,
While beach balls float without a care.
In every puff, a secret's spun,
The air is full of summer fun.

Laughter dances on the waves,
As sandy toes do wild raves.
Conversations fly, oh what a scene,
With wind and sea, it's quite the routine.

So let us chat with breezy cheer,
As jokes get tossed and tickles near.
With every gusty banter shared,
In this vast ocean, all are paired.

Embracing the Gentle Uplift

A light caress upon my nose,
As kites take flight in funny poses.
The laughter of the leaves above,
Sings sweetly of this playful love.

Squirrels dance on branches tight,
With acorns rolling, oh what a sight!
Each gust brings silly jive and twirl,
The trees nod, a leafy whirl.

Floating by on breezy waves,
My hat takes off like one who raves.
Chasing down my runaway cap,
Is this a jog or a windy lap?

So let's embrace this playful lift,
With breezy hugs, life's greatest gift.
As chuckles swirl and joy ignites,
We ride the wind through day and night.

Fluttering Heartbeats of the Afternoon

In the garden, petals cheer,
As the butterflies flutter near.
With a breeze that tickles noses,
I laugh at all the silly roses.

Dandelions dance, oh delightful spree,
As floaty seeds escape with glee.
They bounce and sway, a funny crew,
With every gust, they go askew.

An ant parade joins in the fun,
With tiny heels that weigh a ton.
They march along the windy lane,
Comically, they stake their claim.

So here's to hearts that leap and play,
As afternoon skies colorfully sway.
In this fluttering, breezy show,
We find the joy in every blow.

Portraits in the Air

Clouds drift by, creating art,
A fluffy dog? A jelly tart?
With wind brush strokes, so absurd,
A painting made without a word.

The sun giggles, winks with light,
As shadows dance, a funny sight.
A gust draws smiles on every face,
In this gallery, we find our place.

Leaves draw pictures, twist and twine,
In the whimsical, intertwining line.
Each breeze brings laughter, light, and cheer,
In this portrait park, we gather here.

So let us paint the skies up high,
With colors bright that never die.
In every whisper, flicker, stare,
Life becomes a portrait in the air.

Leaves Whisper Wishes to the Sky

Leaves dance and sway with glee,
They tickle the clouds, oh so free.
Whispering secrets to the bright sun,
Hoping one day, they'll have some fun.

With each rustle, a giggle escapes,
In a world of tree-hugging shapes.
They play hide and seek with the breeze,
Cheering for squirrels and chasing the bees.

Nature's gossip flows, never stale,
Branches gossip about the snails.
Telling tales of a wandering lark,
Who thinks he's the king of the park.

A flutter here, a sneeze from a flower,
"Oh dear, did that bee just devour?
A petal or two in his brash flight,
Silly bug must think he's a knight!"

Secrets of the Enchanted Draft

Rustling whispers from the tall grass,
A playful draft, like a cheeky lass.
It tickles the toes of passing ants,
Dancing around with frolicsome prance.

"This way! That way!" it calls to the leaves,
Spreading laughter as joy it weaves.
Mossy old rocks giggle with delight,
Caught in the mischief of day and night.

A secret exchange, the winds conspire,
To send the clouds on a poetic quire.
With fancies afloat, they spin and twirl,
Amidst the enchantment, they giggle and whirl.

Who knew fun's a matter of style,
Dancing along each inch and mile?
Nature chuckles, all with a wink,
As the draft whispers and begins to think!

Messages Carried in Each Sigh

Whispers flutter on the air's soft sighs,
Brief notes from daisies to surprise the skies.
"Did you hear? The sun just lost its hat!"
And the daffodils chuckle at that!

A sigh of the wind holds secrets inside,
Like a gossiping breeze caught up in pride.
Each huff and puff carries tales from afar,
Of a cow who thinks it's a shooting star!

Trees take turns with stories to tell,
Pines gossip sweetly, while oaks know it well.
They share little quirks with the squirrels that pass,
Playing charades with a crackle and sass.

With every puff, the air sparkles bright,
Each sigh's an adventure in nature's own night.
A comedy sketch in a green, leafy guise,
All wrapped up neatly in puffy disguise!

Hues of Nature's Breath

In the garden, colors collide,
As the wind paints with whimsical pride.
Hues of giggles in flowers abound,
Every petal's laughter echoes around.

Dandelions fluff, like puffball clowns,
Decked out in yellow, with whimsical gowns.
They sneeze in the breeze, a playful event,
Spreading laughter wherever they're sent.

The lilacs chuckle as they sway in style,
Waving hello with a cute little smile.
While the roses blush, feeling quite grand,
In their regal tones as they take a stand.

Every shade a story, vibrant and bright,
In nature's palette, there's pure delight.
So here's to the colors, alive and absurd,
In laughter and joy, their voices are heard!

Gentle Zephyrs Through Eden

In gardens where fruits giggle bright,
A wind tickles leaves, playful and light.
The flowers dance with silly delight,
As whispers of joy spark laughter in flight.

A butterfly flirts, wearing a grin,
While bees, in their buzz, join right in.
They pollinate dreams with pollen of fun,
In this merry symphony, joy's never done.

The trees wear hats made of fluffy cloud,
As squirrels hold court, feeling quite proud.
They chatter and tease from their lofty spots,
In this easter egg hunt for all the warm thoughts.

With each gust, a chuckle is found,
As daisies throw parties all around.
Nature serves punch, laughter aglow,
In this whimsical world where spirits can grow.

Embrace of Celestial Air

The skies are painted with a jester's hue,
As air courts the leaves, promising new.
Clouds spill giggles like soda pops,
While horizons stretch like a ballerina's hops.

Gentle breezes tease limbs, light as twine,
Tickling grass blades, making them whine.
Dandelions puff with a playful cheer,
Sending wishes afloat, far and near.

With sunshine winking, the day's just begun,
As nature plays tag, everyone's won.
A frog leaps in joy, sporting a crown,
In a kingdom of laughter where no one's a frown.

Each whispering gust is a playful jest,
As cool currents swirl, offering rest.
In this game of chase, hold on to your hat,
For the sway of the air brings giggles like that!

Tranquility's Soft Caress

The gentle hush of a breezy sweep,
Caresses the hills while everyone sleeps.
A raccoon rolls over, dreaming in glee,
While crisp leaves recount tales of the tree.

Whispers of wind flirt with passing birds,
As trees share secrets—no need for words.
The sun plays peek-a-boo, hiding with glee,
A joyful game that is fun as can be.

With each rustle comes a chuckling sound,
Nature's own laughter, swirling around.
The daisies compete for the best-funny face,
In this playful show, there's always a place.

Clouds drift by, like soft marshmallow dreams,
As ice cream cone sky drizzles sweet schemes.
In this charming embrace, mischief at hand,
Joy blooms abundantly all over the land!

Lullabies of the Summer Sky

In the cradle of summer, breeze plays its song,
With whispers of laughter, the days stretch long.
The grass leans back, feels ticklish and free,
While clouds giggle softly, floating like tea.

Each petal's a giggle, bright colors they fling,
As moths and fireflies come out to swing.
A butterfly winks as it flutters about,
In a glorious festival of fun and no doubt.

The stars blink in rhythm, a cosmic delight,
As crickets compose their tunes of the night.
With every soft sigh, a joke takes its place,
In this symphony woven with laughter and grace.

In these lovely moments, nothing amiss,
As breezes blow kisses, offering bliss.
So sway with the tunes of the playful skies,
And find joy in the laughter, beneath twinkling eyes.

www.ingramcontent.com/pod-product-compliance
Lightning Source LLC
Chambersburg PA
CBHW072217070526
44585CB00015B/1382